Mommy, Tell Me About African-American Inventors

Never stop learning!

Written by G. D. Bowman

Illustrated by Anita D. Randall

This book is dedicated to my loving parents, the late Dr. Ollie Monroe Bowman, Jr. and Mrs. Gaynelle Cohen Bowman, who ensured that I learned to appreciate the art of writing at a very early age.

To my beloved daughters, Sterling Noelle and Carmen Alexandra; and my granddaughters, Ayla Marie, Aliyah Monroe, and Grae Noelle, may this book inspire all of you to seek more information about your African-American heritage. It was written with love.

For children everywhere... and those who read to them.

"Hi. I'm Sterling, and this is my little sister, Carmen.

Mommy told us that African-Americans made lots of things that help make living easier… and many of those things are right around our house."

"Look Carmen! There are some things right here in our kitchen that African-Americans invented--the refrigerator, the stove, and the mop! Even potato chips were invented by an African-American by the name of Hiram S. Thomas. Well, I think he had a little help, but I know he was at least one of the inventors."

"Mmm. I love potato chips," said Carmen as she munched on one.

"And Dr. George Washington Carver who was once a slave, became a famous scientist who made hundreds of inventions out of sweet potatoes and peanuts," boasted Sterling.

"If you look out the window, you can see lots of other inventions made by African-Americans. There's the lawn sprinkler, the mailbox, and the lawn mower. I'm proud that our people made so many inventions."

"Are there other things around our house that African-Americans invented, Sterling?" asked Carmen with excitement.

"Oh yes!" There's Mommy's old typewriter, the dryer, a fire extinguisher, the ironing board—even your old baby carriage."

9

"What's a typewriter?" asked Carmen. "Oh, it's what old people used to type on before they had computers," answered Sterling.

"Really? I can't imagine not having a computer! Tell me about some more inventions," begged Carmen.

"Let's see… oh, I know! See that clock on the wall? An African-American man by the name of Benjamin Banneker made a clock out of wood that lasted 40 years. He also loved math and astronomy, which is, well you know, the study of the universe. Hmm, let me think of some more…"

11

"Hi girls. What seems to be so interesting?"

"Mommy, I was just telling Carmen about all the great inventions that our people helped to make. You know, like the stove, the dryer, the refrigerator, the ironing board…"

"And don't forget about the potato chips," interrupted Carmen. "Would you please tell us about some more, Mommy?"

"Sure. Every time you're riding in a car, remember that the traffic light was invented by an African-American man by the name of Garrett Morgan.

"And automatic elevator doors were invented by Alexander Miles."

The first pencil sharpener, a fountain pen, and some of the advanced electric lamps were also invented by African-Americans, as were many of the things we see, touch, and use every day. Unfortunately, African-Americans weren't always given credit for their inventions, and some of the history was not properly recorded."

"That's not fair!" said Sterling. "But I'm sure glad to know about those that are right here in our house. I'm proud of our people. They really did contribute to the building of our country."

"And yes, this little gadget was invented by an African-American man by the name of George Grant," added Cousin Leah as she walked into the room, holding up one of her golf tees.

"I guess he realized how hard it would be to drive the ball off the grass," she chuckled.

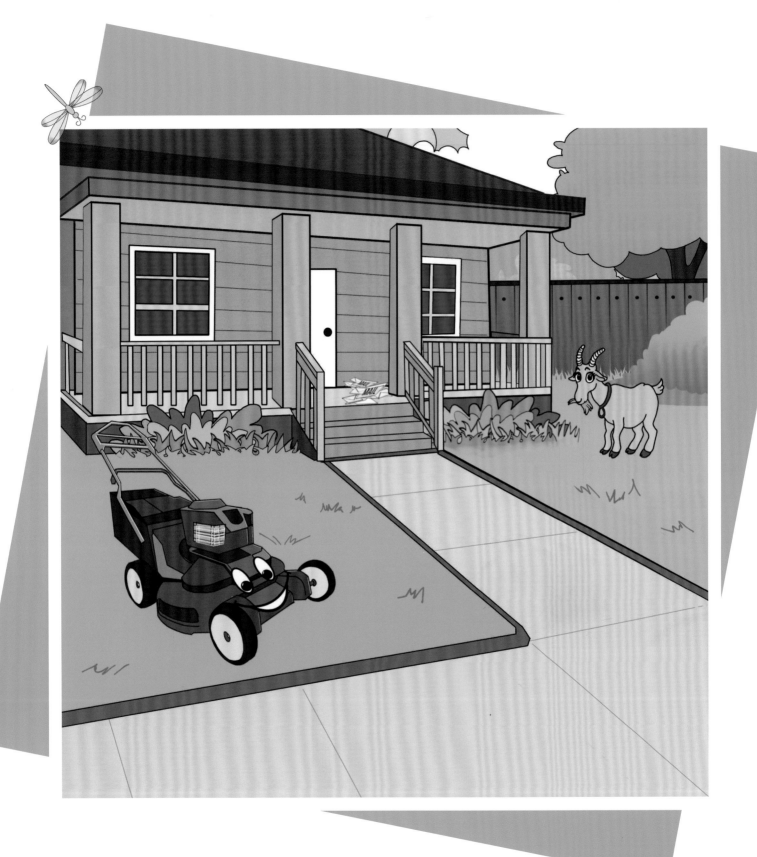

"Can you imagine how tough things would be if we didn't have some of these inventions?" Mommy asked. "If we didn't have a mailbox, our mail would be stacked up on the porch and without a lawnmower, we'd have to get a goat to eat the grass! I am so grateful for all of these inventions that African-Americans made."

"You got that right. Without them, we might be telling time by the sun, and cooking by an open fire," said Cousin Leah. "Come to think of it, we'd probably be cleaning the floors on our hands and knees, and that would just ruin my manicure!"

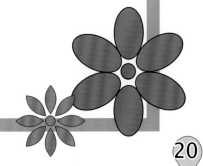

"Gee! When I grow up, I think I'll invent something!" said Sterling.

"Me too," chimed Carmen, "Me too."

22

The End

African-American Inventors In This Book

Automatic elevator doors*	Alexander Miles	1887
Baby carriage*	W.H. Richardson	1889
Clock*	Benjamin Banneker	1753
Clothes dryer (U.S. Patent)	George T. Sampson	1892
Electric lamp*	L. Latimer & J. Nichols	1881
Fire extinguisher*	Thomas J. Marshall	1872
Fountain pen*	W.B. Purvis	1890
Golf tee	George F. Grant	1899
Ironing board*	Sarah Boone	1892
Lawn mower*	John Albert Burr	1899
Lawn sprinkler*	Joseph Smith	1897
Mailbox	Philip Downing	1891
Mop*	Thomas Stewart	1893
Pencil sharpener	John Love	1897
Potato chips	George Crum	1853
Refrigerator*	John Standard	1891
Stove*	John Standard	1889
Traffic light*	Garrett Morgan	1923
Typewriter*	Lee Burridge	1885
Various inventions	George Washington Carver	Early 1900's

* Improvement or variation of original invention.

Be sure to visit your local library or conduct internet searches to learn about other important inventions by African-Americans.

Color this invention. Can you name the inventor?

27

Color this invention. Can you name the inventor?

Color this invention. Can you name the inventor?